Stop Turning Screws With A pipe Wrench

1

Earl B. Smith

Published by Earl B. Smith, 2023.

While every precaution has been taken in the preparation of this book, the publisher assumes no responsibility for errors or omissions, or for damages resulting from the use of the information contained herein.

STOP TURNING SCREWS WITH A PIPE WRENCH

First edition. June 17, 2023.

Copyright © 2023 Earl B. Smith.

ISBN: 979-8218215231

Written by Earl B. Smith.

Table of Contents

Preface

———

"**A**lthough there are plenty of people who can fix things, there are not many who will fix things correctly."

This was a statement I made to my friend Frank, an entrepreneur. He hired a contractor to install new windows on his rental property. After they were finished, they notified him, and he went to review their work. On the surface, the window installation looked great, but his wife took a closer look at the work. She noticed flaws in the way that some of the trim was installed. Frank showed pictures of the finished work to me. I was appalled. I agreed with his wife. They installed new aluminum over a damaged wood frame. I felt bad for him.

The year before, he hired a remodeling contractor. After the contractor finished the job, the basement drains flooded. He brought in a plumber and the plumber found the drains filled with drywall debris and paint. It is likely that the remodeling crew had been pouring debris from the wall repair down the basement utility sink. The debris hardened and blocked the drain. I was upset and embarrassed since I had referred Frank to that contractor.

I have hundreds more stories like these. Contractors are supposed to be skilled tradespeople but become a customer's worst nightmare. Regrettably, this truth is not confined only to contractors.

Imagine the chaos that would follow if we learned that an aircraft mechanic or an auto technician was careless and unconcerned about their work. They carelessly left bolts loose on the engine. Or if you found out that the technician at your local water department habitually lied on preventive maintenance paperwork and now the city has thousands of citizens gravely ill from the polluted drinking water. This is simply indefensible. However, this kind of malfeasance is occurring all the time.

There have been many disasters of failed infrastructures such as bridges, water supply systems, railways and building collapses, even in recent news reports. Why are there more stories like these? These are usually the result of bad maintenance habits. One bad act by a maintenance or service person can cause so much pain for others.

My father was a parts inspector for a bolt manufacturer. They made bolts used in the airline and car industry. He says, "almost" - don't make it. It's either right, or it's wrong." His emphasis on accuracy helped influence my concern when repairing or installing equipment. My dad believed in precision. I learned how to read precision tools, like micrometers, when I was only 12 years old. I didn't like it back then, but it helped shape who I am as a professional technician today. He also believed that quality should be at the core of how every person performs their duty.

I am what people refer to as a *maintenance man*. I'm grateful for the career path I chose. I have met great people, all while providing service to those in need. Like my dad, I take my career seriously. I can fix anything. The more experience I gained, the more skills I acquired.

Dad was serious about his place in the world also. His HVAC business spanned over four decades. The vast number of his early clients did not have large budgets, but he still managed to give them quality work. He also taught me that they were willing to pay for great service. He never wavered in his efforts to provide all his customers with high quality assistance.

I enjoy teaching people how to service the equipment of others. Whether it is repairing a homeowner's swimming pool or a manufacturer's production line machine, qualified people are vital. A technician's approach can make or break a process. If your heart is not in it, then you will not execute it well. To be successful you must not have a half-hearted approach to the work.

My dad hates the term "handyman." He sees the description as a derogatory term. He says it is reminiscent of an uncanny TV handy person that conducts temporary fixes only to return and fix them again. Their unprofessional antics often make them the most laughable characters on the show. Sadly, it's a correct depiction of so many real-life technicians in the field today. I collaborated with some people like this in my business and career.

I wrote this handbook expecting to persuade you to care about the work you perform. Hoping that the principles herein will get you focused on perfecting your skill and your standards. The world thinks highly of skilled people like you and me. During the 2020 pandemic, they coined us "essential workers." We help keep the world moving, eating, sleeping, and building capital. This book is my way of straightening things out. My hope is to guide all techs to perform like a professional.

Earl Smith, M.P.A.

About The Author

For 15 years, Earl B. Smith was a residential electrical subcontractor, working on various pieces of equipment in the most important places and companies in America. His career spans over 30 years, with a background in heating, ventilation, and air conditioning systems, working as a millwright and an industrial mechanic in hydraulics, pneumatic systems, high voltage electrical and robotics. He is also a former member of the International Union of Operating Engineers, Local 18-S.

After graduating high school with a certificate in Building Maintenance systems, Earl went on to earn a bachelor's degree in Sociology and then a master's in public administration. He spent a few years as an instructor and program director at a technical college but spent most of his career working in the building and industrial trades.

Earl did not expect to spend his life getting his hands dirty. He originally wanted to be on a stage entertaining people, singing, and performing in places all over the world. Instead, Earl was with his dad repairing refrigerators, freezers, and furnaces. During his youth, He was right by his father's side, learning about the honor of servicing the needs of people, and how to perform like a pro. His father had once told him, "If you're determined to do this entertainment thing, you must have a backup plan." Fortunately, the backup plan became his main plan.

Before We Begin

The points I make here are intended for any person that repairs or services anything. This includes the tailor or furniture reupholsters, airline mechanics, people that repair jewelry or computers, cable TV installers, and even the cell phone repair person. All of us have a vested interest in serving the public well. It is upsetting to find shoddy repair on a furnace. It's just as devastating to find out the tailor did a terrible repair on your daughter's wedding dress. We should abide by a set of principles that help create a quality standard.

A technician or a "tech" fixes or installs equipment that is supposed to make life easy for their employer.

A professional worker (pro) is committed to their role and strives to give their best effort in performing their skills. They are committed, dependable, certain, and knowledgeable. They operate under a sense of excellence. A pro is dedicated to applying high standards in every area of work.

Our employer is the person or organization that compensates us for performing a service or executing a task.

The scope of work we provide comes with a mutual commitment. We agree to fulfill our duty to our employer, armed with a serious mission, the proper tools, a skill set, and a professional perspective. In turn, the employer commits to compensating us for the work we do. Sometimes, we are compensated with money. Other times they give us things. I remember when I was given a woman's late husband's tools. It was her way of giving me a bonus for the work I performed. I made sure to fix all the things on her list. She was grateful and I was, too.

I want to help the installer, maintenance person, millwright, mechanic, and service person in any field. It is my desire that after you read my book and practice my suggestions, you will be thorough and conscientious in your work, and able to build value in your services.

Every person that services, repairs, or installs anything should have standards. By this, I mean an outstanding approach to how they accomplish their duties. I see this as doing the work in a way that keeps the employer happy while creating further opportunities for the service worker's business or career.

There is no centrally recognized national code of conduct and work standards in the repair and maintenance industry. Often, an experienced, seasoned tech develops a set of habits that are ingrained in their memory, a sort of muscle memory. Their habits may be good or bad. No matter what, this book can help you improve. If you are new and still developing, you have not learned bad habits yet. I am sure I can give you a positive perspective.

Quality Service

If you are a maintenance person working at the mall, a service technician at the vacuum repair shop, a tailor, or an airplane mechanic, your finished work tells your story, and it determines whether you are a pro or not. Throughout the years, I held myself to a set of guidelines. These guidelines beg a few questions. First, have you done quality work? Is the customer satisfied that you gave the best care to their equipment? Secondly, are the customers comfortable with your skills? Do they have confidence that you know what to do to fix their problem? Third, does the customer feel safe? Have you left them in an unsafe place? Finally, what is your attitude? How do you approach work and the people? Given all of this together, I call it the QCS and A fundamentals.

My father's business spanned over 40 years with a slew of satisfied repeat customers. For over 30 years, I used the same focus on customer service and quality that he used. The following are the commitments that guided my work.

Your first commitment is to give the customer *quality service*. When a customer hires you, they entrust you to do quality work. It should not be solely reliant on how much money you're earning. Every person deserves our best effort. The work we do reflects our own values. It is like when we make an appointment to see a medical doctor, we expect them to take great care of us. If they do not give us their best service our symptoms could worsen. Again, we should always provide quality service.

Quality insists that you apply your best effort. Here is a personal experience of a discussion I had with someone new on the job.

Tyler was a new hire. I had not interviewed him, but he had an impressive resume. The hiring manager felt he would be a good fit and placed him in my team. I assigned him to small projects just so I could observe his work. Within the first few weeks, I discovered he was not a good fit at all. Most of his work had to be done again by another technician.

After a month, he had amassed a set of incomplete tasks, and his finished work was sloppy. In addition, he had a lazy attitude. On some occasions I had to motivate him away from his work bench. Eventually, the other department managers requested work to be done by anyone else but Tyler. In time, he quit. I suspected he recognized that he lost my confidence and the trust of his teammates.

Whenever I talked to Tyler, he had an excuse about the reason his work was below expectations. He said he felt that his work was unappreciated. I could hardly wait to make the following point to him. I said:

"If a customer feels that you are giving them subpar work, they become leery of your skills. They are less willing to continue paying you for it."

If you work for an establishment and enough people notice your sloppy work, you will earn a reputation for being unconcerned and unskilled. This leads to a lack of trust and respect for you and your skills. This affects when you get raises and when and if you will get a promotion. If you are self-employed, of course, the customer is your employer. We are in the era of social media and the ability of real time posting. Unsatisfied customers will go as far as taking pictures of your poor-quality work and posting them on social media. They will also post bad reviews online. An abundance of dissatisfied customers will ruin your business.

Our customers depend on our commitment to doing quality work. For instance, the manufacturing industry earns money when their equipment is functioning. Hotels earn revenue when the rooms are adequate for guests. The fitness gym is ready for business when the weights, pool and the air conditioning system are working. Neither of these businesses can function properly unless we provide quality service.

Quality demands a thoughtful plan - Every Screw Counts.

Normal habits of a handy person include stuff like having screws left after finishing an office desk from Walmart and throwing the extra screws in the kitchen drawer with the rest. However, they find the furniture flimsy. But it works well enough to place appliances on it. If you have not done this, I'm sure you witnessed it. Repeat after me, "Every screw count" To be a professional, you must develop thoroughness. The screws are not "extra!" When you have screws left it means you missed something. What harm will it cause?

An inexperienced technician on the first shift found screws on the floor underneath a rotating shaft. They found the set screws loose and tightened them. The bearing looked good, and there was no other damage. So, they picked up the extra screws and threw them in with the rest of the assorted screws and bolts on the shelf. Ten minutes later, the shaft picks up speed and a small vibration occurs. After a few hours, the vibration increases.

The unit was violently shaking. The second shift technician arrives and notices the noise and investigates it. They discovered that the set screws were loose again on the collar that was recently tightened. A coworker speaks up and says that there should be additional locking screws on top of the existing set. He said that a week ago they installed additional set screws on top of the original set. The extra set were intended to lock in the others which continued to loosen.

First, just because you have knowledge and experience does not mean you will make the right decisions. In this case, both technicians have poor working maintenance practices. Every screw counts! It's not about the screws, it is about the why? Why were the original screws inadequate? Why were the screws loose in the first place? Why was the unit vibrating? And finally, why didn't either tech do anything about it? There are actions that each tech could have done to resolve the problem. The first tech failed to give the information to their coworkers. The second tech should have pulled out the screws and inspected them. Leaving a unit in this condition creates other problems and will create more damage to the drive motor.

When we accept the responsibility for a project, whether it be a repair or an installation, we also make a promise that we will leave it in the best condition based on its design. Our knowledge or experience should guide our every step. We have the use of all our five senses in helping us do thorough work. What do we see? hear and smell? And in some cases, how does it feel? All equipment has manufactured recommendations. If we read the factory recommendations, they can help us home in on a solution to a problem when it occurs. All these are tools we should use to finish our task correctly. To be the pro. Our employer is relying on us.

Quality demands and approach - Hide the sledgehammer.

It is customary practice to use the wrong tools. Like an uncle that uses pliers to pound in a nail sticking out of the porch flooring; or the neighbor that uses a butter knife to tighten a screw on the loose door hinge. But as a professional, when we use the wrong tools, it threatens our commitment to quality. Take for instance the use of the sledgehammer. We would be shocked to see a surgeon enter a surgical unit with this type of tool. I am equally nervous when I see a sledgehammer in our work. It is rare that we should use one. Yet, for many technicians it is the "go to" tool. Certainly, the sledgehammer is an essential tool, but it is often a tool that creates havoc. Some people don't know how to use it, and there are others who do not know when to use it. Why am I making a big deal out of a sledgehammer? Well, when we use heavy force, it says that you have exhausted all other means. Yet it has been my experience that this is usually not the case. The use of force should only be used when all options have been completed. Professionals have the knowledge to make the simplest decisions. This decision separates the amateurs from the professionals. And it should. Unfortunately, pros make the same mistake.

> *Years ago, I was yelled at by a rigging contractor. I borrowed his rigging chains to relocate a platform. I was unaware that the chains were the wrong kind of chain and hook for that specific type of rigging. Unintentionally, I was stretching the chain. He yelled and swore at me. I was not happy about it. But looking back, I deserved his wrath.*

The pipe wrench is a similar tool to a sledgehammer. It is intended for use on pipes or in a circumstance where all the other methods for gripping and turning have been exhausted. Still, just like the sledgehammer, a pipe wrench leaves abrasive marks on equipment. The point here is that an unprofessional person tends to force things. Normally, the use of additional force is an indication that all else has failed. The pro applies the right tools and the necessary force to get the job done. The unprofessional tends to lean toward quick-and-easy and applies force immediately. **Please don't be that person!** Whenever I teach or coach a new technician, I make it a priority to stress that details matter. I say:

> *"If I picked up my Cartier from the watchmaker, I don't expect to find scratches on it because it was placed in a vise."*

In another familiar example. Look at the wall at your friend's home. Notice the streaks in the paint on the wall? This was caused by applying paint with the "wrong tool." The painter used a brush instead of a roller. It won't matter, until the lighting in the room highlights the imperfections in their house. We are responsible for taking care of people's important assets. Part of being a pro is the ability to be both proportionally gentle and rugged. There is no one-size-fits-all when it comes to our approach. Like I said, use the right tool for the job. Do not make the job more complicated by using tools that make matters worse and, at the same time, make you look like you don't care.

Service is the purpose of our work. We must keep that in mind from the time we start a task until the task ends. Whether you have a business working on vacuum cleaners or are an industrial mechanic in a foundry, we get paid to fix things. When repairs are completed, the customer does not expect to have to worry about paying for the same repair again. Every piece of equipment we touch is important to its owner. It should be important to us. To you, it is a 15-year-old washing machine. To the single parent with three kids, the used washing machine helps keep her white scrubs clean. She cannot miss a day of work. Your complete repair aids in her earning enough money to take care of her children. When you show up to repair it, it's like she hit the lottery.

Quality demands permanent fixes.

Be careful, temporary fixes become permanent disasters.

A leaky gas line had been damaged for at least two years. The gas line was hidden inside a basement tool shed. Luckily, I was there to repair the furnace and noticed the smell of gas. There were two elderly people in the home.

I was running new electrical from the basement to the attic. I ripped up the floorboards and saw a ball of wire wrapped in duct tape. Under the tape was a set of stripped wires without wire nuts, held together by additional pieces of duct tape.

* *The finishing company clients included aerospace and automobile manufacturers. The company assessed for fatigued points of the metal products like axles and drive trains. The process included shooting 25 mm sized metal beads at 40 - 60 psi. A hose exploded while one of the workers was using the blast equipment. Thankfully, the worker was not injured. As I inspected the damage, I realized that the hose was heavily wrapped in duct tape. Under the tape was a larger hole. The ruptured hose had been repaired earlier with wraps of duct tape.*

There are no temporary repairs. We are paid to fix things.

The public perception of duct tape is a picture of a loosely wrapped car riding along a downtown city street. The average person will not have a role in their possession. But unfortunately, techs use it. That boils my skin. Here's why. Duct tape is used in place of missing brackets and bolts, and to cover up cracks and dents. As a maintenance manager, I forbid my team members from using duct tape. Sure, I have some in stock. But it is in my office hidden in my desk. I once threatened to fire someone for using that tape. I insisted it should be strictly only used on duct work. Which is what it is intended for.

Unfortunately, when duct tape is used wrongly it is not removed and the repairs are never done. Because it's overlooked, hidden by the duct tape. Then when the damage gets worse, it is too severe to repair.

Duct tape is one method used by a lazy person. It is an alternative way to temporarily fix things. My wife says, "Lazy people do the most work." In her view, if you do not do the job the right way the first time, eventually the work must be addressed again. Whether it's duct tape, flex seal, or some type of metal epoxy repair. This holds true. These tools should not be in our toolbox. It is presumptuous for me to expect that there is never time for short-term repairs. But even brief fixes should withstand certain quality standards. Remember, when we fail to do our job, we breach the end of the agreement.

Things to consider when making temporary repairs:

- Ensure the patch job has an end date.

- Immediately schedule a permanent solution and stick to the date.

- Document the interim repair as well when the follow-up will take place.

- Frequently, check the fix and document the progress.

- Would you trust this repair in your home, or business? Confirm the repair is adequate for the job.

- Use the correct material or industry rated product.

In closing, when you see quality as your goal, that stance will add to the strength of your work. It will help your work publicly stand out. It will help you push for the next best step. Finally, because I understand that the word "quality" may not mean the same to everyone, let me explain how I see it.

- Be thorough. Finishing the task is your goal. If you can't finish what you start, then don't start it. When you agree to do a job, think of it as a verbal contract. You must deliver on your promise to complete it, otherwise you are in breach of the contract. You should not expect to be compensated for unfinished work.

STOP TURNING SCREWS WITH A PIPE WRENCH

- Ask yourself, is it what they paid for? If not, this is another area where you have breached the silent contract. If your goal has not been met, then you fell short on your end of the deal.

- The finished work should be pretty. It should make you proud when you stand back and look at it.

- Cleanup. Pick up debris caused by your work (a customer panics if they see pieces and parts left from the task).

- Are you ready to sign your name on it? If you will not swear by your work, then you're not a pro.

Comfort With Service

———

The second commitment is our promise to provide *comfort* for the employer. The goal is to make their life comfortable or better by using our skills to solve their problems.

It wasn't his fault.

Pastor Dennings was furious when I arrived. He hired a repair person to put up ceiling fans. When he left their home, Mrs. Dennings noticed that some of the electrical plugs in the house did not work. Mr. Dennings said he noticed that the repair person was struggling. He observed that the ceiling fans were crooked and making noise when they were spinning. Eventually, Dennings asked the man to leave, and he made the decision not to allow him back to do more work. In the past, he witnessed the handyman's shoddy work.

He ignored it, he said, because he had not damaged anything. Still, Pastor Dennings lost confidence in the man's ability to do large tasks. He relegated him to doing smaller ones. He called me and said "Man, come figure out what this fool messed up." I went through the house and discovered many electrical issues. After two hours of tracing wires, I uncovered a broken wire behind the wall. This was an area far away from where the repair person had been working. Turns out, despite his poor workmanship, the loss of power to the plugs wasn't his fault at all. His only flaw was that his past poor-quality work in the past set him up for anything else that went wrong.

An employer is left uncomfortable when they lose confidence in your ability to do the work. They dismiss you and your purpose. This is a terrible but familiar scenario. If a technician has a lazy approach to their work, it creates a bad report and thus any tech with a bad record is deemed unqualified.

The comfort we bring relieves the worry of our employer. Get this, if a tree is falling and leaning toward the house. When you show up with a truck, saws, and tools, they breathe with a sigh of relief. They anticipate the tree will be cut down and removed, saving their home from damage.

We provide comfort when we solve problems. They entrust our experience. In this, it shows the importance of earning a good reputation. When people have good things to say about your skills, it is evident that you are doing the right things. If they have bad experiences with us, then we have work to do. If you are lucky enough to receive their trust, don't mess it up. Work your butt off to meet or exceed their expectations.

Shoddy and shameless!

The window company showed up to replace the windows. When my business partner and I arrived the next morning, we saw the old, discarded windows laying in the grass next to our property. The workers were gone. When we called to report it to the company's office, the person answering the phone treated our complaint like it was a minor mistake. They promised they would arrive in a few days to clean up and remove the windows. Instead, it took them three weeks and another six months to install the rest of the windows. But only after I sent them a scathing email.

We determine whether a task is completed. I think of this when I enter an office space and look at the new ceiling tiles. However, there are two left unchanged from a water stain. The unprofessional believes that the job is complete because most of the tiles have been changed. The room looks better. But the task is far from done. Let me explain. First, there is still one or two stained tiles left to replace. Second, where is the source of the leak? The job is not completed until you find the source of the leak and contain it or fix it. Or else, the water finds its way back to stain the new tiles. The argument from the rookie is I wasn't given the duty to make the fix. My response is either you are lazy or clueless. This is indisputable. The employer expects that all the tiles will be new. If their expectations are not met, then the task is incomplete.

As a young tech, I was tasked with winterizing. One task was to turn off all water fountains in the facility and remove any water left in the lines. Well, I overlooked one. An entire section of offices was flooded, and some expensive tiles and wallpaper were damaged. At the time, I argued that I was sure that I had turned off all the fountains. I made a list and checked it twice. But given the outcome, I was wrong.

The late Senator Daniel Patrick Moynihan said: "You are entitled to your opinion. But you are not entitled to your own facts."

Yes. indeed. I was suspended for three days but that day I learned a valuable lesson. The words of the pro should be trusted. In my case, it was just an upset season ticket holder with a flooded loge box. But what if the flooded water happened in a children's hospital or a fine art studio?

Our employer may have limited knowledge about our jobs. It is critical that our assessments are sound, the finished work should be flawless. This creates comfort in our employer. When techs perform poorly it creates a paranoid public. Our employers or customers are busy watching us work just to make sure we do not trash their stuff. I think of the senior customer who watched me install lighting throughout his apartment building. I was there all day. He was there, too, sitting on a chair in front of every work area, staring and questioning the process. I was not angry because I understood his skepticism. The last contractor ripped him off.

Your best work will be ignored the moment someone witnesses haphazard work. A custom reupholster who does inferior work will not be in business for long. Good workmanship cannot be taught; it must be learned and ingrained in your psyche.

Here are my last tips on this. The following is how you can avoid doing shoddy work.

- Learn the correct way of performing a task, then commit to doing it that way until you have mastered it-then you can do it your way.

- After you have finished, stand back, and look and ask, "Can I put my name on it?"

- Pour your soul into your skill and it will return the favor

- Learn as much about your craft as you can from other people, books, school, and other resources.

- Be anxious to learn. Strive to become an expert. Do not turn down a chance to grab credentials. I know people who are great at what they do. But they have no respect for pursuing credentials. In their mind their skill set is enough. Credentials help pave the way for you to access more experiences. If I can't prove that I was formally trained to work on cars, then it's rare that someone will let me work on their $75000 luxury car.

- Be eager to work along with others with more experience in the subject.

- Be open-minded; try other ways of doing certain work with the goal of becoming sharper.

- Be humble. Practice your craft in humbleness, knowing that there is always something new to find out. Whenever I was too confident, I stuck my foot in my mouth. Bragging about how good you are is only shining light on your future mistakes. I made fewer mistakes when I kept an open mind.

- Do not be afraid to admit what you don't know. In our line of work, guessing can damage equipment or cause you or someone else physical damage or death.

Safety With Service

―――

Another striving toward pro status is our commitment to *safety in our service* - Our employer expects that they will be safe during and after we do the work. Again, they assume we know what we are doing. They trust we have the knowledge and experience. This perception provides them with assurance. They assume the work we are doing is safe.

Harold worked with a group of contractors on a remodeling project. He oversaw capping discarded gas lines. After the job was completed, the father smelled gas and discovered Harold had not tightened and sealed one of the caps leading into a bedroom where the man's daughter slept. Luckily, he found it, and everyone was safe. The General Contractor never used Harold again.

Throughout the years, I've seen many cases just like this. People disregard the protection of others to make money. I witnessed this with contractors and coworkers. It is our duty to leave our customer in a safe condition. Every time a person touches a button on a machine that we repaired, stands on a step we installed, or turns on a gas stove that we fixed, their lives are in our hands. Safety is a mindset. One that must constantly be updated and matured as we continue in our field.

Safety takes Time.

It was a 2004 Ford Explorer. It was in good condition when I bought it. I purchased it from one of my closest friends, Derrick. He was an experienced mechanic. It seemed like a great buy. However, within a year, I started having problems with the truck. Derrick usually came and helped me. Like the time the gas tank fell off at night as I left the nightclub. It was late, but

Derrick arrived with his tools in hand to make a temporary repair so that I could get home. Later we replaced it with a used one from the junkyard. Not long afterwards, the door latch was broken for the rear hatch. I wasn't really concerned with this since I rarely used it. I worked many days of overtime which is why Derrick usually did the repairs. For a while, the truck ran without any issues.

Then the brakes went out. The master cylinder was bad and some of the brake lines were rusted. I was not going to spend too much time repairing the entire system. I replaced the damaged brake lines and placed a used master cylinder on it and put the Explorer back on the road. The next day the lines leaked at the master cylinder, and I couldn't stop the leak. I took it to Derrick's shop, and he worked on them for a while. He managed to slow down the leak, but more work had to be done. I had an interview later the next morning and I did not want to be working on the truck all night. I told him that I would pick up new lines after the interview.

The next day, I hopped in the truck and headed to the interview. I sped down the street and twenty yards from my house, I hit the brakes around the steep curve. As I pressed the brake pedal, the pedal went straight to the floor and the truck was not slowing down. Instead, it was increasing in speed as I was going down the hill. I was terrified. I thought about the emergency brake but did not have any faith that the system would work. As I came to the end of the curve, I saw the trees and bushes. I braced myself and drove directly into them.

The truck came to a sudden stop. I sat there for a few seconds. I was afraid that I would be fatally injured. There was a city worker across the street cutting the grass. He slowly walked over to the truck and peeked and asked if I was, okay. He later told me, "You hit that tree so hard, I thought you were dead." Luckily for me, I survived with no injuries.

I look back on that incident. It serves as a personal reminder to prioritize safety in quality work over inconvenience. When we are held responsible for equipment it is more important that the equipment works at its best. A temporary fix is often unsafe or damaging overall. I know there are times when employers usher us to hurry and make quick repairs. It's the company who strongly urges us so that they can run to meet quotas. Or it's a customer who tries to hurry repairs because they believe the work is taking too long. You will always be conflicted with having adequate time to make safe repairs. Despite this, keep your commitment to safety and quality in the forefront of your mind.

Of course, there are times where compromise will become necessary. In your commitment to quality, you should work to find common ground without forfeiting the level of quality. Unfortunately, if you work for an organization, it means you must periodically alter your work hours to fit operating needs. Be open to doing that. If you are the owner of the business, be bold enough to turn down jobs that will not allow you the time to keep your first command to quality. Under every circumstance, do quality work. Remember, rushed work translates into quick and sloppy repairs. Two or more poor repairs create constant emergencies and escalate a maintenance work backlog. It also creates a dangerous condition for equipment and for the equipment's operator.

Look at this:

In 2022, Tesla recalled 24,000 Model 3 vehicles for a "safety" recall because a belt anchor that was not refastened after a repair was made on something else.

In 2020, General Motors had a safety recall on several Chevy, GMC, Buick, and Cadillac. The vehicles were missing bolts on the start/stop accumulator end cap.

Luckily, there are no reports of deaths because of these missing attachments. This oversight was likely from an assembly line worker. This emphasizes my point that everyone should have succinct training if they are servicing or installing "anything." The assembly line worker believes that they are just placing hundreds of parts on a chassis every day. In fact, they are securing the safety of the customers. The customers drive the cars that their company sells. To this point, I passionately believe anyone that services or installs equipment should have similar standards applied to their roles. I believe my QCS-A fundamentals will help keep people safe. The assembly worker does not require the same training as the maintenance person. However, they play a crucial role in their company's commitment to safety.

In February 2023, a train derailment occurred in East Palestine, Ohio. The Norfolk Southern train was carrying toxic material when thirty-eight cars derailed and caught fire. The accident devastated the small community of 4700 people. Initial reports discovered that a wheel bearing had over-heated.

"This was 100% preventable." ~ Jennifer L. Homendy, chairperson of the NTSB

Guardian.com reported on a leaked audio from 2016, a former Union Pacific Carman said that she was encouraged to avoid marking bad bearings in need of repair. Her manager mentioned that it would increase the time that a train is not moving.

This type of passive view of safety has become pervasive throughout multiple industries. A pro commits themselves to working safely. When you leave work unfinished, sloppy, and unsafe, or ignore procedures or protocols, it shows that you are not ready to be considered a professional.

There are no mistakes, just failed plans.

Two times I bought the hot surface ignitor to repair Mrs. Sales furnace. The hot surface ignitor is the glowing orange colored component that creates ignition to the gas burners for gas stoves and furnaces. It helps create the spark for the fire. The first ignitor I bought. I installed it, and it didn't work. After 45 minutes of troubleshooting, I discovered a hairline crack in it. This prevented the electricity from flowing through. Making it unable to glow. I thought I was careful. But I bumped it against the frame of the furnace burner as I was replacing it. The second ignitor I purchased did not work because I touched it with my fingers. There is a note on the directions with a warning that the oil on your hands causes the ignitor to malfunction. I rushed back to the supply store and got a third one. Eventually I replaced it and fixed the furnace. However, after I left her house, in my haste I lost the money rushing into my car to head to class. I was working in the daytime and taking a college class at night.

One common cause of mistakes in our field happens when we fail to adjust to adverse conditions. So here is a quick note:

When we find that conditions are different, we must do something different.

For instance, When I arrived at the home to repair the furnace. I discovered that the basement had very little lighting. It was even darker near the furnace. I ignored what I saw or what I could not see and did the job anyway. I could have easily run out of the truck and grabbed my work light before I started working. Then I would have been able to see and could have avoided hitting the component against the burner frame, or I would have noticed the crack in the component.

Another cause of what we call a mistake is when we hurry. There is an adage that says, *"Haste makes waste "*For example, on my second try, I was aggravated because I had been there so long. I rushed to get the job done and ignored the handling procedures. A procedure that I had typically followed.

There is a whole lot I can say about rushing through tasks. Especially work that requires a meticulous approach. However, the bottom line is that often our work takes time. If you do not have the time to do the job right, don't do the job at all.

Darnell's work painting homes was highly praised. He painted the entire second floor of the house on Hillvrest avenue. He had not ordered the paint himself, but trusted there was enough primer. However, when he started on the back wall he ran out of primer and continued painting without applying it. Two days later, the customer called and complained that the last wall seemed to be a different shade than the rest. Darnell was not happy, he returned to paint the back wall again. This time he applied the primer before he painted over the blue wall.

Darnell's failure was two-fold. First, he purposely decided not to use primer on the last part of the walls. Although he knew primer was necessary when transitioning from darker to lighter walls. He also failed to stop painting when he realized that he did not have enough primer. His mistake was that he failed to make sure he had enough primer to finish the job before he started.

This third scenario outlines an additional problem, take ownership of your work to avoid mistakes. Taking ownership of your work requires that you organize the job from start to finish. If you are teamed with anyone, it is your job to make sure that person is on the same page. Once you take on your role, you acknowledge you are in full control of your work. If you fail to do that, then you failed the customer.

Sharron's issue

She drove her car for two years. It was her first new car. She loved it. She enjoyed the great gas mileage. A new gas station opened in her neighborhood, and she purchased the same grade gas as she does every two weeks. The next day, her car shut down and sputtered. She took it to the mechanic, and they discovered that her fuel system contained too much ethanol. They drained the system and the gas tank and refilled it with gas that contained less ethanol. What she learned is that the manufacturer recommends that her model Kia Sorento should not use gas that contains more than 10% ethanol content. After she learned of this, she recalled seeing a green sticker on the front of the gas pump before she pumped the gas. The decal read "may contain more than 10% ethanol".

She acknowledges the ethanol sticker, but she had no training in mechanics and had not read her car's manufacturer book. However, she was on the hook for paying the mechanic for the work her oversight caused. This was a real mistake, albeit a costly one.

This brings us to another cause. Failures can occur if we fail to apply the correct information. In Sharron's case, she was not aware of the information. Therefore, she could not foresee the problem. In Darnell's case, it's common that painters will avoid using primer, it takes time. His problem occurred because he was aware of the information but failed to use it.

No mistakes allowed.

The direction in performing precision work comes with directives. One of the written specifications looks like this, +/-. This says this metric doesn't have to be perfect, but near perfect. This is the way we must operate in our field. Mistakes will happen in our work. Even when you have the best work standards in mind. However, we should minimize the mistakes. Both David and Sharron's mistakes created problems that were easy to solve.

However, more catastrophic things can happen when technicians make similar mistakes. Still, small mishaps can prove fatal when the work involves critical pieces of equipment.

Below is a list of common missteps I personally witnessed throughout my thirty plus years in the maintenance service field. In each situation my team and I were able to correct the problem and move on. In comparison, in some well-known cases though, similar mistakes were made that had catastrophic consequences. I avoid naming the public disasters due to the sensitivity of these public incidents and the lives that were affected.

- The wrong O-ring was installed in the fuel system. The o ring was not rated for the operating temperatures of the equipment.

- Improperly rated metal supports for concrete structures.

- Inadequate power industrial vehicle lifted a load too heavy.

- Inadequate power industrial vehicles used for the wrong application

- The use of sealant in an enclosed space (improperly ventilated)

- Concrete anchors installed with weak epoxy

- Improperly torqued bolts

- Motor leads are not fastened tightly

- Sensors are left partially wet or dirty after initial checks

- Failing to see that the circuit fuse was too small

- Failing to see the circuit fuse was too big

STOP TURNING SCREWS WITH A PIPE WRENCH

Unfortunately, to see news stories where failed plans produce huge disasters. Help me to minimize my own mistakes. I am methodical but cautious. I've been accused of being paranoid. Rightfully so, I recognize my responsibility. I'm convinced that being over-precautious will make you a better technician.

Finally, What I have discussed in this section concerns our own personal convictions. Please strongly consider adapting them into your heart and mind.

- Take your role seriously.
- Do not be afraid to evaluate your own work.

- Do not skip a step because you think the step is unnecessary.

- Become a promise keeper.

- Promise to be serious about your role.

- Promise that the work you do is the best in your ability.

- Promise not to take shortcuts.

- Promise to hold yourself accountable for any failures you make.

- Promise to learn from them.

Please take these measures to evade safety missteps.

- Follow proven protocols. Consider that there may be things that you don't know. By following procedures, you avoid making reckless decisions.

- Do not ignore what you see. By accepting the truth of what you personally observe, you can determine what your next step should be.

- Tell the truth on paperwork - record keeping is useless if it is not factual.

- Trust but verify, a line I borrowed from our former President, Ronald Reagan. Do not take chances on your safety or the safety of others. It is dangerous to work on a live electrical system. It is also dangerous to assume that the water is shut off when you are working on a leaking water line

- Before you work on any equipment or device, turn the system off, verify it is off, isolate the system so it cannot be turned back on (yes, it's a lock and tag out procedure).

Everything we touch can bless others or create harm for them. We are servants. We serve people by fixing their problems or by finding "safe" solutions. We live in an interconnected society; one person's actions affect another.

A Servant's Attitude – Elements to Serve

The final demand for us is in the way of our *attitude*. When I talk about attitude, I am speaking about how a tech approaches things. How we process tricky situations. How we see other people or view the work we do. People who maintain a good attitude can perform well no matter what happens. For instance, a tech must see the old broken equipment as salvageable and recognize its value to the employer. To become a pro, it is important that you develop and maintain a good attitude. I worked with a person that had a bad attitude. He found everything wrong with the world and rarely had anything good to say about anything. Although he occasionally laughed, he was a miserable guy. He was knowledgeable and he worked hard but people exited the room when he showed up.

Accept the role you play.

Jim was a passionate carpenter. He could build a room fast. He was young, gifted, strong, and smart. He had great ideas. He rarely complained about his job. Part-time, he built decks and sheds for a small selective clientele under his own business. However, full time, he did roof and wall framing for a large custom home building company. They enjoyed having him on their team. They could always count on Jim to give his best efforts. His supervisor, Harold, thought highly of Jim too. He was impressed with Jim like everyone else. Although Harold liked Jim, he thought Jim was often overly concerned about decisions that the company made. Harold dismissed the comments. He suspected that Jim lacked an understanding of how a business works. Nevertheless, Harold saw that eventually Jim could be his replacement when he retired.

Then suddenly Jim quit. Through a text message he announced that he was resigning immediately. They were sad to see Jim go. His diligent efforts contributed to the company's success. Harold suspected Jim drew frustration with the company's management. He did not agree with their decisions. However, the company moved on, without Jim.

If you own your business. You create the business based on your expectations. The rules fit your vision and are part of your plan. Anyone you introduce to your business should be given a specific role to play. Their skills should support your vision. In the same way, when a company hires you. They expect that they are employing a professional. One that will support their goals. Even when you are the best employee, your purpose in their company is in supporting their objectives. Just as it would be if you hired a professional worker to work for you.

Foremost, no! The customer is not always right. Instead, I believe, the customer is paying. Moreover, it does not matter whether you judge them right or wrong. Your assignment is to provide **your** best service to them. A pro satisfies their clients requests and needs. Their requests take priority over what **you** believe.

Accept your role – play it well.

Often, coworkers tease me for going beyond the scope of my job description. That is because I believe that those who work in service, repair and maintenance should not work like they are alone. Our work has partners. We are interconnected. Just like a company's shareholders, we should be engaged and attentive to our partners. If we fail to do our job it can have adverse effects on a company's daily operations, revenue, future, and staff.

I took a flight recently and thought about the maintenance issues that may be associated with things like repairs and replacements of customer seating. In an airline, all the stakeholders benefit when the seat is repaired. First, replacing a seat on an aircraft is more serious than going to the junkyard and removing a seat from a car on pedestals and installing it in the family car.

There is more to think about. The FAA and other government agencies place mandates for seating. These same mandates extend to the person making repairs. Take for instance, an airplane seat on one plane cannot necessarily be replaced with another without consideration. One major consideration is in choosing a seat that is specifically for a particular aircraft. The seat manufacturer designs and builds the seats to accommodate weight limits for a particular plane. Obviously, because weight can affect the planes' elevation and altitude. The manufacturer must also think about the customer's comfort. An uncomfortable seat can be a nightmare for an airline.

Our work is important. If the company has a nightmare, it is shared pain for all the people involved. We should continue to be committed to performing our tasks in a manner that says that we accept our role, and we will play it well.

I think about the NFL stadiums executive who stated, "Don't be bigger than the thing." It will not matter that you are smart, talented, and work long hours. If you have abandoned the reason you were hired. A sense that the relationship should be a mutual one. You perform the work they want, and they compensate you for it. Our work is better performed when we are passionate. Unfortunately, that same passion will entice your ego. Gradually, your ideals become more than your service. Again, there is honor in serving the needs of others, especially when you are getting paid for it. It is dishonorable to want your needs met and become unwilling to meet theirs. It would be like the vegetarian that works at McDonalds for six months. Refusing to serve their hamburgers because they do not trust the meat. In this scenario, McDonalds is not the bad actor; they kept their end of the bargain.

But what if you are a contractor that owns a company?

Say, Mrs. Robinson wants you to do work that violates your personal principles and standards. The answer is it is not too different from what I stated in the last paragraph. Still there is a mutual understanding. Except, you have the right to refuse to serve anyone for any reason. In this case, you must also refuse to accept any payment from her.

Since our skills are used to service equipment. We are service workers. That makes us servants, that's just the way it is. When I worked as a youth worker in church, I placed the focus on delivering information and caring for their spiritual well-being. I served with a heart of passion, commitment, and love for what I was doing. To assist people, you must harness the ability to serve. You must believe there's value in serving others. Indeed, there is value in installing a light fixture in the dark backyard to help with a homeowner's security. Or replacing a defective proximity switch to keep the factory production line running. Commit to a willingness to serve. There will not always be someone there to show their gratitude for your work. You may not always be properly compensated. I take the cue from my dad. In some cases, he was overpaid for his services. In others, he was deeply underpaid. But in mentioning these things he would always end by insisting that he would give them the best service anyway. Being internally equipped with a servant's mind requires the ability to see excellent value in helping people.

I worked in a recycling plant, a multi-level apartment building in the city, and an NFL football stadium. My focus is always on what the organization deemed as important. We are ineffective when we lose sight of our function as a service provider. You may be an industrial mechanic servicing line equipment in a factory. Or an appliance repair person servicing home appliance. Or a boat mechanic offering services to get an inboard or outboard engine fixed so its owner can get back in the water. Your skills help achieve the goals of others. If you take offense at being characterized as a servant, then you should find another career.

The bad

The apartment manager had a tech replace our thermostat and it wasn't working correctly. A service technician showed up at our door early. My wife asked him to take off his shoes or wear booties to protect the carpet. He said, "Well, I never do that." However, he complied. As he walked over to look at the thermostat, she commented that my husband thinks the problem is with the new thermostat. He told her "Let me figure out what it is, I'm the service person." I don't think he noticed that I was sitting at the dining room table.

At first, I remained quiet and continued listening. I was unsure if he was joking. He mumbled something under his breath while snatching the cover off the thermostat to check on the batteries. Suddenly, I jumped up and grabbed the door, opened it up, pointed to him, and said, "Get your ass out of here, nobody talks to my wife like that!" He looked stunned. I said it again. This time I added, "If you don't leave, I am going to help you." Trust me, he left.

Sadly, the people with the worst dispositions desire to work in roles that provide service to the public. A person with this type of demeanor will not perform well around others. There were many encounters with people like this, including unpleasant doctors, nurses, home remodeling contractors, landscapers, appliance repair people, mechanics, and electricians. If you have ever been criticized for being like this, stop it! Seriously, you need to change. It is impossible to be considered a professional if you consistently have a negative demeanor. It means that when you have added stress you will only get worse. It's time to make the correction, an evaluation on your mental health. Of course, not every person that behaves this way is mentally ill. But what I am suggesting is that the person should have a mental evaluation to get to the root of their unacceptable behavior. This requires deep introspection. Self-examination is hard because it forces us to admit who we really are as opposed to who we portray.

I was teaching a class on electrical boiler controls. Kim was one of my students. She complained to the director that I repeatedly passed her up for team lead assignments and that she believed that I was unfair in my grading scheme. She accused me of having a vendetta against her because of her bad attitude. Conduct she openly admitted. Usually, she was arguing with me or her classmates. While she accused me of disliking her, she also acknowledged that occasionally I gave her accolades. Also, I helped her with difficult assignments and was lenient with her during challenging projects.

When she had outbursts during class, I would pull her to the side and warn her. I told her that her attitude frightened her classmates, and the conduct would be detrimental to her grades and her career. She informed the Director that because of her "past acts" I penalized her too much on her grades and class positions. In the end, the campus director stood by company policy. Which left the grading standard and class projects to the discretion of the instructors. Kim wasn't pleased but she stayed in school and graduated. A few years later, I ran into one of Kim's former classmates. They told me they hired Kim to work on a rooftop air conditioning unit. Kim started yelling when the customer questioned her about a method she was using. Of course, she was fired.

People that bring bad energy to work only make the task more difficult. It creates unnecessary intensity. For example, one person may be having a difficult day. The duty for the day gets complicated. Every person is getting frustrated. Since there are no positive and calm minds there to associate with, the task suddenly creates an unbearable environment.

The Good

A few years ago, I had a second interview for a maintenance director's job. At the opening of the meeting, the hiring manager said that after my first interview, I received multiple professional references from a few of their present employees. I wasn't sure what she was saying so I asked her to explain. She described that her assistant was the former hiring manager for one of my former employers in the rubber and plastic industry. She brought along a few of the production workers, too. Ironically, I remembered the company and the experience, sadly it wasn't one of my fondest memories.

It was 2008 and the economy had taken a dive. Good paying jobs were scarce. However, this company was doing plenty of hiring. Two days before my first workday, they informed me that they would pay me less money. Still, I took the job. I didn't like the working conditions. The building had no heat for most of the winter. There were raccoons and mice in the building. The floors were made of worn old wooden cobblestone. Some of the sinks and toilets weren't working. Often there were little or no paper towels or toilet paper. Most of the workers were overworked and underpaid. Strangely, the coworkers came to work with a smile. We all recognized that the economic conditions in the country left many without jobs. Sometimes when things were slow, I had to work alongside the production workers helping them with their work. However, we were all grateful to be working and we made the best of it.

After my initial interview, my name came up and all of them remembered working alongside me. They talked about how much they liked me and how grateful they were for the help I gave them. Now, some ten years later, they were sharing my great attitude with people I was meeting for the first time.

A good attitude will follow you. Having a good attitude is the pathway toward doing remarkable things. It is a result of how you perceive a certain moment and what you do with the experience. Take the guy I met that specializes in bespoke clothing (custom-made). He told me stories of the clients that refuse to pay him. Garment companies use his designs without compensating him. Yet, he is still at it. In fact, he is a highly recommended and a requested tailor. He is a little more cautious these days but still gives his clients discounts. I've never heard a disparaging word about him from anyone. What he said to me is "It's what I do."

Every day is not going to be a breeze. In the same way, bad days will not last. Our role is to solve problems for other people. Our attitude and our workmanship determine whether our employer considers us valuable. If you are a contractor, it means you will have committed customers that will be devoted to your company. If you are an employee, a good attitude means you are likely to be recognized for promotions, raises, etc.

In closing, keep a positive perspective. Perspective is in how you see things. First, to maintain a good attitude, you must have a personal commitment to be at your best. Look at every day as a privilege to serve and to use your skills and get paid. Yes, you must be grateful to be used. Yes, I'm saying it. People use you. Your skills are valuable. So far, they

STOP TURNING SCREWS WITH A PIPE WRENCH

have made the way for you. The reward is in the pleasure that you bring others. It may sound corny, but it's the truth. I stood by this view for many years, and it works.

It can be challenging to sustain an optimistic attitude. I worked through it all, miserable and lazy coworkers, bad supervisors, less than favorable working conditions, low wages, heavy and complicated workloads, extreme outdoor and indoor weather. After spending my younger years as a stressed-out tech, I made a pledge that I would tune out external forces so that I concentrate on what is important to my needs. Life consists of duplicating the energy you bring. You receive what you bring to the table. You still must fulfill your promise while all these factors are taking place. Just as you expect to get paid for your work, your employer expects you will give them what they pay for.

Forget what you know.

The blower motor had suddenly stopped working. I suspected that it was a fuse. So, I ran and retrieved my multi meter from my toolbox. I pulled the fuses out of the holder and checked them. I found that all three had blown. The first thing I did was match the amperage specifications on the nameplate to make sure they were the proper fuses. At first glance, the fuses were rated too high for the motor specifications. However, when I spoke to one of the lead engineers, he informed me that the fuses should be much higher. I was perplexed. In my experience, the current fuse rating was already too high.

At first, I was ready to take him to task and give him a lesson on amperage ratings and motor protection and all that stuff. But then, I remembered the shock I had as I looked over the electrical prints a few weeks back. Although I have spent many years reading schematics and ladder logic diagrams, the prints looked foreign. I was unfamiliar with the listed components. I had not seen them before. What I learned was that these higher fuses were purposely installed. Briefly, it was to accommodate the inrush current.

As I replayed this experience it persuaded me to take a different approach. "Plainly, there is a new way of doing old things." Since then, I've thought of myself as an experienced apprentice, temporarily shelving what I know. My view is that given today's younger, smart and internet savvy people, there is always a new way, a new technique, some unknown ideal or information of which you aren't aware. Saving energy, time and the preservation of natural resources are the biggest drivers of technology. If you have been doing things for a while, there is a tendency to get a little overconfident. If you're not careful, self-confidence will persuade you to jump to conclusions and create a scenario where you appear clueless. When a tech appears ignorant, they become ineffective and untrustworthy. Our duty is to convince people we can help them. We must be careful not to do anything that could jeopardize their faith in us.

The Executive Vice President met with all the stadium staff including the building engineers' team, the team in which I was serving. Lou spoke of the responsibility we all had in shaping the fans' experience. In short, he explained that when we are doing our jobs and have a willingness to help others do theirs, the fans will have a great experience. He noted that things like trash blowing around the stadium can be picked up by office staff, building staff, or any of the executive's staff. He says, "Please don't be bigger than the thing."

It's not work to me, instead, it's part of playing ball.

There are various methods of tackling certain problems. The approach matters. I call it playing ball. Really, that's how I approach the work. Using a sports analogy, it's easy to comprehend.

If you play any kind of sport such as baseball, football, or basketball, then you know that skill is only part of the game. Just like a ball game, there are fundamental rules. Otherwise, you will never be able to land the ball where you want. The goal in our work is to bring the job to a close but as a proper fix.

Milner had a bombastic attitude. He had sharp skills but not the skills required to play positions in which he often volunteered. His coworkers knew that and shook their heads whenever he did it. He had a tough time finishing everything. He was often too lazy to think things through. Or he lacked experience or knowledge and was too proud to admit it. He shoots in the dark. He shoots without aiming often, never landing the ball anywhere that matters.

In other words, he rushed to fix things without a plan or the plan he had was riddled with assumptions. For instance, he solved problems by cutting wires or changing parts without thoroughly diagnosing the problem first. He usually ran out of energy and couldn't get many things done. Probably because he either didn't have the knowledge or lost the enthusiasm. However, he always found someone to finish it. Milner worked hard but often wasted a lot of time.

On the other hand, there is Eric. He also volunteered for positions he didn't have the skills for. But Eric studied the game. He sought advice from everyone. The people who rarely made the winning shot and the people who are known for their accuracy.

He waited and worked hard. Eric didn't burn out. He tried the shots over and over, making notes of what he did wrong. Until finally he found his groove. Then, he posted up, aimed then fired. Eric excels on every team he's on.

Just like playing a game on a basketball court, more precision is needed when you try "long shots." Remember what I said in the beginning, "There are plenty of people that fix things but there are not many people that fix things correctly." There is more to just having the technical skills to perform a task. There are other essential contributors that make it likely that you can become a pro at this. Skills like critical thinking are a vital element of this work.

Let's look at the term "troubleshooting." Today a troubleshooter refers to a host of professionals including those who diagnose machines, trade pros who find solutions to problems that occur in their field. But in its origins the term troubleshooting or trouble-hunter was an early 1900 term that referred to those who serviced the telegraph and telephone lines. They had to locate then fix non-working communication lines. Imagine how challenging that must have been. In the 1900's there weren't many established roads that you could travel on. Additionally, horse and carriage were typically the means of transportation. This meant that the workers had to be accurate. To be accurate they had to have full knowledge of how the system operated. Any error they made in figuring out the problem could mean more traveling. Which could delay other repairs in other places.

Troubleshooting is a skill. As a kid I watched my dad diagnose equipment that predated him. Back then, he was still learning. We spent hours tracing out chard wires from an old boiler. Often with little lighting and temperatures below zero. In the end dad found the problem and fixed it. Time after time, no matter what equipment he took on, I witnessed him go through the same process.

Learn: Use any source to gain information.

Locate any written documentation. Sometimes, the only written documentation I was able to track down was worn schematics or handwritten notes. Whatever you find will help provide information for the process. One handwritten note on a schematic saved me a day's work. Of course, when you show up at a person's home to repair their dishwasher there will hardly be any information. But the internet is a perfect source for anything. My point is that don't make a habit of just jumping into a fix without having information. For instance,

A woman had water spilling under her sink after she finally decided to use her newly installed dishwasher. Her kitchen was remodeled, and they added a garbage disposal and the dishwasher. After a day of the water leaking, she hired a plumber. He cleared her kitchen drain. She ran the dishwasher after he left and had the same problem. She called me, I was working in the apartment building where her friend lived. When I looked at the problem, I had a thought. I asked her for the paperwork on the dishwasher and the disposal. Suddenly, there was a diagram and description in both the manufacturers paperwork. A drawing showing the plug in the garbage disposal. With a note that read "Please be sure to remove the plug before installing the drain for the dishwasher."

Listen to anyone with any information.

This was a lesson I learned twenty years ago as I started at a window and patio manufacturer.

One of the operators was quiet and reserved and didn't talk much. I was dispatched to their machine and discovered that the machine was not operating. They couldn't tell me what went wrong because they had just returned from using the restroom. They asked if I needed their help, but I declined. (I often think better when I have no distractions.).

After an hour they returned. I still hadn't found the problem. Then they asked, "Did you look under the table? I said, there is nothing under the table that should interrupt the machine starting. So, I continued tracing out wiring on the other side of the wall.

After 15 minutes, I followed the wiring to a box next to the machine. Underneath the machine was another set of wires above a storage box. I saw a smaller box dangling from the two wires. Finally, the operator appears and says, "That's the thing I was talking about."

It was a stop switch that had been hit and dismounted. It had been fixed and became a nuisance, so the operators tucked it out of the way. In their haste, they must have pushed it in. A point they were trying to make to me before I dismissed them earlier.

Now, my very first day on the job is usually spent with the person that operates the equipment. Or the customer that calls to complain that their unit is not working. They know more about the equipment than anyone. They can tell you how it performs under normal conditions. They can explain what doesn't work well and what they believe is the reason it fails. You will avoid being frustrated and save time by applying useful information from the people who are most familiar with the equipment.

Observe

By manufacturer's design, the equipment should function the same way most times. This consistency is a benefit to the tech. If you observe its functions enough, you can predict its operational sequences. It may be a watch, a manual or automatic garage door or even an x-ray machine. Trust what you hear and see and even smell. When it is over you will know it. For example, the motor on a garage door opener makes a different noise if it's struggling to pull the door up. A sign that the door is off track. Don't let it go until your curiosity has been calmed. There were times when I'd be on the hunt for what I believed was out of place. A coworker nicknamed me the hound dog. I acknowledged the term, I never stopped until I found the problem.

Record

Don't expect that you will remember what you did the last time a problem occurred. The best practice is to make a note someplace detailing what you learned. I tucked notes on a file on a computer or on a note app on my phone. Usually marking the file "lessons learned." Or you're like my dad who still writes stuff down. In any case, it is ridiculous to go through all the trouble and learn new information then lose track of it. The lessons you learn will help when you're trying to solve problems with other equipment.

I carried my lesson learned spreadsheet with me from employer to employer. Interestingly, I also have notes from when I was a contractor that has helped me find solutions as a maintenance technician. This will help you develop your own personal "how to" book, a new resource from which you can draw.

Mastery attracts other masters. Opportunity will find you.

We learn from every job that we perform. With every nail we strike, we become better at hitting it dead on. With every screw we torque we get a better feel for tightening them. For this reason, I disagree with the popular term "jack of all trades, master of none." It depends on your personal motivation and determination. If you desire to be an expert tradesperson or tailor and you are willing to do the work, you can achieve it. Your internal motivation should drive you toward your best. Hopefully, I've shown you how to frame your actions and intent. People become good at what they practice. Therefore, every work you perform will generate a solid standard, no matter what job you're doing.

I took advantage of the opportunities that were presented. We should take on roles that expand our knowledge and technical know-how. This gives us broader appeal. Dad started off fixing washers and Dryers and later became a residential and commercial hvac contractor. I started my career working on home air conditioners. I advanced my skills to include working in AC/DC currents, motors and controls, welding and fabrication and machine troubleshooting. This type of progress is necessary. Most times I was unsure I had the skills to take on the responsibility, but I was too curious to turn it away. I continued to learn, master the skill, and win.

> *My sister Shay was an infant when she was introduced to the work dad was doing. He placed her in the truck in her car seat, and he traveled to his service calls. She sat right in front of the air conditioners and boilers as he was working. At the same time, she was also watching as her mother participated in buying real estate. This provided her with a plethora of experience by the time she was an adult.*

> *My sister was less interested in lugging around tools. Instead, she chose to go into managing properties. Her approach was different. She earned the job by volunteering to work for a property management company for free for a certain period. Now she travels from state to state taking care of other people's property.*

It's been said that Picasso made some 50,000 works during his lifetime. Thomas Edison's visions helped him acquire 1,093 patents. This tracks what I believe about the law of progression. Which explains the benefit in maintaining the ability to stay on the course. Build on the skills that you acquire and then take advantage of the opportunity when it is presented.

STOP TURNING SCREWS WITH A PIPE WRENCH

In summary:

- Become a student - always be open to learning something new about what you already know.

- Be committed to continuous improvement - whether it's by attending seminars or classes online or at a training college.

- Stay with an open mind. Be willing to listen to the ideas of others, even people that don't have experience in our background.

- Avoid arguing what you think you know unless you are asked - there is a small opportunity you may be misguided, which can be disguised as ignorance.

- Serve through humility.

- Don't be bigger than the thing.

- Play ball.

- Learn, observe, record.

- Boldly go where your skills take you.

Finally, when people are satisfied with your skills, they will, in turn, make sacrifices to compensate you for the service you provide. If they see you as a troubled, unorganized, lazy, or incompetent worker, they will reward that, too.

The Making of a Professional

———

This section of this book is for those who are contemplating whether they should enter the service industry. Maybe you wish to start a business replacing people's gutters. You repaired a few for friends and family and now you're passionate about it and believe you have a good thing. Or you're attracted to the shortage of repair and service workers in the industry. Technical knowledge is one of the requirements of our job. A carpenter should know how to read a tape measure. A person that repairs copy machines should have knowledge of the different toners and how to change them on a copy machine. But there are also other considerations.

Let us look at what it takes.

First, as I have already mentioned, it takes a service attitude. I've talked a lot about the act of service. I mentioned it frequently because it will be a fundamental part of your daily routine. Take the idea of calling a plumber when your toilet is clogged. Unfortunately, there is only one in the home. While I am using the example of the clogged toilet and the responsibilities of the plumber in the scenario. The same requirements can be said for those who want to fix gutters or heavy equipment or air conditioners.

When you call the plumber, you expect that they are responsive. Responsiveness covers a multitude of areas, including communication. There is more to add to this list. Since you will be working with the public. Every word, action and behavior are important to your success. Do not take any of them lightly. Coworkers were denied raises for being lacking in their interactions with superiors or to customers. In our work first impressions really do matter. Customers will not let you in their home to do anything if you cannot communicate with them. They would be leery of the totality of your skills if they see that you are impatient. Or if you cannot figure out what to do next. Or you can find an alternative path that works for them. I will go into more detail in the new book. Please stay tuned. For now, below are a few points on what it takes. These are must-have skills.

A. **Effective Communication**
- **Relevant Knowledge**: When a person calls in a panic. The person answering the phone must have knowledge of what you are calling about. The response must be coherent. What I mean by coherent is the response must include knowledgeable and well-thought-out answers. The way to learn proper knowledge is through formal education or a training program. Whether it is a union apprentice program or vocational college. Successful instruction should include hands-on training, but it will also include classroom work, reading, writing and math.
- **Considered listener**: Considerate listening demands that the speakers' concerns are met. This is the basis of being responsive. You must listen to them well to fulfill their requests and be ready to give relevant feedback. No matter how much training you have, you cannot service equipment if you don't know what's wrong with it. That information will come from the people that are familiar with it. This may be the person operating a piece of equipment. Or the millennial who hired you to fix her car. They know more about the equipment than you. Listening starts with being focused and paying attention to the responses. The next step is to offer feedback.

- ○ **Concise speaking**: Yes, of course you must be able to speak, but most importantly, speak intelligently. Equipped with knowledge and with clarity. For instance, tools and equipment parts are called by their trade name and their nicknames. The Fluidmaster in the toilet is the manufacturer's name. It is the fill valve for a toilet. Anyone associated with the work should be able to convey information. It does my toilet no good if the person coming to fix it doesn't know the difference between a compression assisted toilet and gravity-flush type.

A. **Enduring** – Not every toilet can be fixed in a few minutes. This work will take patience. Ironically, you will have to hurry and wait. It is the reason service companies often charge by the hour. Frequently, there are no "quick fixes." I have this saying, "A quick fix creates a quick look." The quick look is my reference to problems that we can overlook. The human psyche loves instant gratification. As soon as we get it, we quickly move on to something else. It's important for a technician to be thorough. They may mean that you must sit there and wait. I've waited 90 minutes for a cycle to finish on an assembly line to find out whether the problem was finally resolved.

A. **Critical thinking skills** (critical thinking) First, what other steps will be taken if the toilet auger doesn't work to unclog the toilet? And what is the next step after that? In many cases the first solution does not work.

A. **Versatility** - Situations change. The person should be able to adjust to complete their task. In this scenario it could include things like repairing the damaged floor around the toilet after the job is done.

Technical skill still rules.

The following writings describe the various levels of a service technician. It describes the temperaments and habits that may be required to fulfill the roles.

Level - 1

The first stage is awareness. As I mentioned, I never wanted to be in the trades, I had other plans. Then I had the natural talent to repair bikes and understand how machines work. It's great when you become aware that you have competence, or an understanding of a certain skill set. This kind of person "tinker" with things. Their awareness makes them popular with friends and family. The fact that they can fix things is beneficial. Their phone is constantly ringing. People invite them to their homes for parties. Suddenly it seems like everyone has a problem for them to solve.

In a 2022 movie called a man named Otto. Otto (played by Tom Hanks) spoke about his passion for cars. I laughed when I saw this scene. I was watching with someone who saw it as a weird exchange. But it wasn't strange to me. As a kid, my dad was Otto in that scene. I am sure my wife will say that scene reminded her of things I've said as we are sitting in restaurants with loud blower motors from the hvac systems that had not been repaired. Or times when I point out a burning mark on an outlet at a friend's house. While some thought it was a little peculiar or nerdy, others took advantage of my skills and gave me a to-do list or offered to go into business with me. The young person that can install and fix car stereos is never short of friends to hang out with. This person has not put thought into the process. They enjoy possessing the knowledge. A lot of people settle at this stage.

Level - 2

The second stage of being a technician is when they participate in official training. They can join their interest with the procedures taught in school or a training program. This step allows a trainee better insight. A welder learns proper welding techniques. The mason learns when to use boning rods or a corner trowel. At this level tech becomes more aware of their capabilities and what paths are possible. They are on track to a career if they want it.

When I was fresh out of technical school and could not get a job in the field, I took a job as a factory porter because it was a position under the maintenance department. After being around the technicians and learning how the equipment functions, I was able to secure a position as a factory maintenance technician. I never looked back.

Technical education gives you a broader awareness. However, it is also where you build many assumptions. At this level assumptions are evaluated. Habits are being tested. This stage separates those who want it and the people that don't. This is the stage where people quit. If they gain the right insight they will stay, learn, and move forward. If they can't handle the criticism, they quit and find other careers and return to "tinkering".

Level - 3

The third stage is the person that has the experience and training. They earned a few years' experience. They are considered trained technicians but at an entry level. This tech has a long way to go. They have not made the common miscalculations. Like the electrician who cut the wire too short and now they need to run new wire. They have the knowledge but not the wisdom yet. This is the phase where accidents are likely to happen. There are two types of technicians at this point. One is the entry level tech who is enthusiastic and ambitious. They take on jobs that seem too big for them. If they manage to exceed the task, they become more emboldened in taking the next step. If a technician continues at this level and avoids doing anything disastrous, they are in a suitable place. However, one unpleasant event will bruise their ego, slow them down and they may even quit doing it for a while. Or go on to do something else. Surprisingly, this person usually believes they know enough to start a business. They print up cards and are usually fine for a while. Although there are few that can hold on. Certain people remain at this level if they can earn a moderate income. But unless they seek more guidance they will collapse because they need more professional experience, knowledge, and wisdom. They are thorns for the seasoned technician because they know enough to get in trouble and can become too prideful to admit their flaws. On the other hand, the apprehensive technician is still unsure of their skills, so they approach things a little slower. If they make a mistake, they take more precautions. They are on track for their next level. They are aware of their limitations and seek to overturn them.

When I was convinced that I wanted this to be my career choice, I poured my efforts into doing what it would take to become successful in the maintenance industry. I wanted to be well rounded. I looked for positions in companies where I could learn new skills.

Level - 4

The fourth stage is the experienced and field trained technician. They usually find their way into another training program. The new program helps them specialize in a certain area. They are more confident. By then they have seen a lot and can figure out how to maneuver around problems. Typically, they are cocky, and assume more than they should. If they continue seeking additional training, they will figure it out. If they learn from their mistakes, they will eventually settle down and continue to the top stage. I have not seen many people quit at this stage. The skills they learn are transferable skills, so if something goes wrong, they can easily head in another direction. For example, I started out as a hvac technician. It was plagued by government mandates, and too many product changes. I chose instead to pursue a career in electrical.

Level - 5

The fifth and final stage is the highly trained, multiyear-experienced technician. To become a well-rounded professional, you will need to be aggressive about gaining knowledge and experience. This person has reached a level of professional expertise. They have a multitude of experiences in various areas and take excellent value in accumulating information. They are patient and humbled by their position in their career. They are also confident but cautious. They seek guidance at every turn. They love challenges. The tests keep them sharp. They usually graduate as senior technicians and after a while they become managers or consultants. Their greatest gifts are patience and tenacity. When you want to be more valuable and more substantial you must do more to be in support of the bigger "thing."

A Little Inspiration

───

This book covers the practices that are needed well after skills are acquired. I focused on the information to speak to the individuals who are already skilled in their prospective careers. However, this section of the book includes a focus on those who are still on the fence about what they want to do with their careers. Or those who may be in transition. All of us need motivation

Commitment is necessary (transcribed from my "Working the Dream" podcast

Skills are not exclusionary. It is the reason that the workforce is missing so many skilled people. Skills are not reserved for any special person. They are earned and must be pursued to be achieved. To achieve a certain skill set, there must be a consistent regiment of focused behavior. Or in other words, a commitment. Unfortunately, we are not born with a concept of commitment. Think about the baby that keeps trying to grab the ball and is unable to grab it. Eventually, they give up and start crying out of frustration. They look around for help.

The point is commitment will develop over time. The achievement is the carrot. For anyone, if they can't see what they will get in the end, they will give up. That is the case with an adult or child. Commitment can be hindered by a lack of insight. Faith, or hope that what they want will come. It's in conflict in a society that wants quick gratification. They are saying, "why should I commit to something that I can't see?" When you grow up you can't think like this. Progress is the act of moving forward. Forward thinking requires letting go of habits that did not yield satisfactory results. Therefore, positive changes are necessary, thus, it's time to make a promise or (commit) to put plenty of effort into changing. Before you commit to anything you need to believe that you can attain what you envision. The first step to attaining a goal is getting started.

There are millions of people who rarely finish anything because they fail to initiate the start. Is this you? People do not have a problem with ideas. They have a problem with finishing ideas. And that is not because something is mentally wrong with them. It is because they have not been taught the importance of finishing.

The act of completing any task is saying, "Okay, I get it, and what is next? "It is evidence of a willingness to go to the next step. It is why we like sports competitions. In basketball we cheer the final shots of the game because we have already looked at what team is next on the schedule. As my father says, "Time to grab the bull by the horn." The winner says, "I'm ready."

Since I was 19 years old, I had a vision. I have operated a business and worked as an employee for great organizations. I provided a service to people. From the little lady in the house in the inner city to the Cleveland Browns executives' employees. I have made a lot of money. All with the same heart in mind. I have an idea, or a service and I want someone to pay me for it. When I felt a hunger to achieve more, I pursued a degree and achieved both a bachelor's and a master's to equip myself for new levels. All the while, being married and raising kids. I am not trying to make this about me and my achievements. My message to you is to push through anything that keeps you from pursuing your dream or trying out an idea. The single most important step in finishing anything is in having the inner motivation to just simply start it. If you start college, you should finish it. If you start a good job, you should get what you want from it before you leave. Keep in mind, to be successful there are things that we should learn. That is, produce a plan. If you get up in the morning, and you cancel thirty things because you lack the time or inspiration, you fail. If you missed your doctor's appointment, you have failed. Because now your health is one week behind.

I read a quote from singer, John Mayer. He says, "If you had started doing something two weeks ago, today, you'd be two weeks better at it." There will always be a reason not to finish or start things. But those excuses are not reasons because they are not reasonable. I say yes, we can acknowledge them. But we cannot continue to give in to what limits us. If you get up in the morning you should have goals that you desire to reach, even if it is a small but important task, like cleaning your house because it helps your mind get going. Just start something and get it done. For change to happen in your life, you must do something different. Something different than what you did yesterday.

Conclusion

———

I hope I sent you in the right direction. As I sat in meetings and interviews with other maintenance personnel, I was often impressed at how well many were immensely trained and experienced. However, once I worked alongside them, I was stunned by their unprofessional and shoddy work. After working a 10-to-12-hour shift, it gets taxing when you find that you must finish job tasks that were left incomplete or sloppy.

When I was a program director at a technical College, I was keen on the students performing like pros. I would say to the staff of instructors,

"Teach them like they will be doing work in your home one day. Yes. I want them to be skilled, but are they going to leave my home a mess when they are finished? Am I going to regret hiring them?"

Build your business and career on giving your best and being on your best conduct. We owe it to our employers, ourselves, and our careers.

Good Luck!

Earl Smith, M.P.A.

maintenanceprofessional@hotmail.com

Search podcast platforms for "Working the Dream" or "Personal Rhythm and Blues" podcast with E.B. Smith

Don't miss out!

Visit the website below and you can sign up to receive emails whenever Earl B. Smith publishes a new book. There's no charge and no obligation.

https://books2read.com/r/B-A-KQQX-UVKJC

BOOKS 2 READ

Connecting independent readers to independent writers.

www.ingramcontent.com/pod-product-compliance
Lightning Source LLC
Chambersburg PA
CBHW060535030426
42337CB00021B/4266